The Tiddler
Sticker
Activity Book

Based on *Tiddler*

By Julia Donaldson

Illustrated by Axel Scheffler

ALISON
GREEN
BOOKS

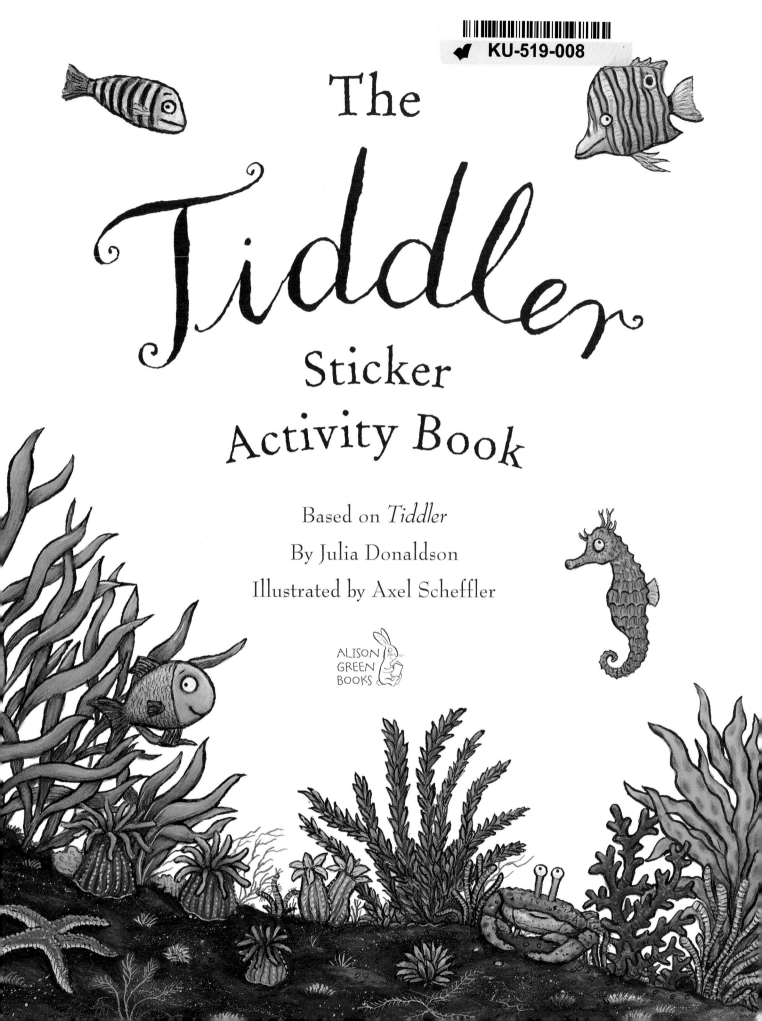

Yes, Miss Skate!

Miss Skate is calling the register.
Can you colour the scene?

Tiddler is Lost

Which line will lead him back to Miss Skate?

A Fish With a Big Imagination

Who can this be? Join the dots to solve the mystery.

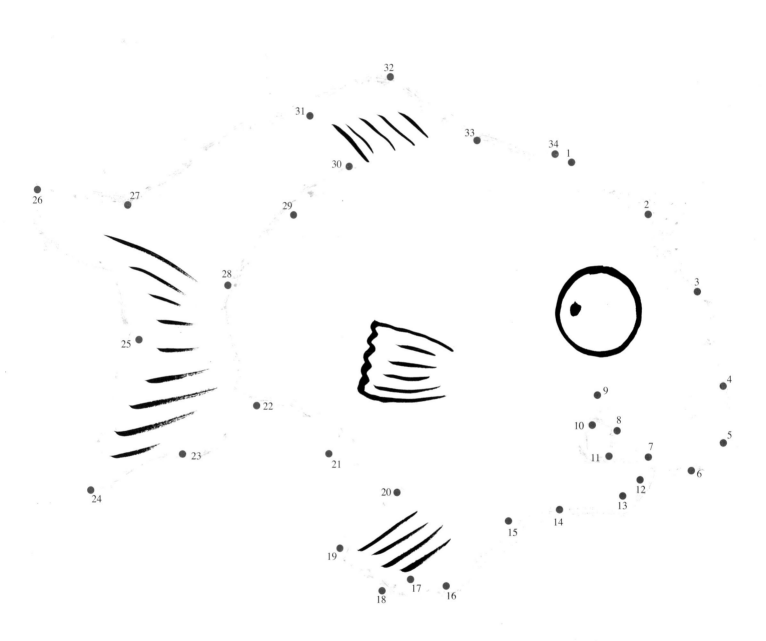

What's Next?

Find the right sticker in the sticker section to complete each of the patterns below.

Sticker Scene

Who's exploring the shipwreck? Use the
stickers to complete the scene.

Drawing Fun

Draw the octopus by copying each square from the
top grid into the blank grid at the bottom.

Tiddler's Wordsearch

There are ten words hidden in this wordsearch. One has already been circled for you – can you find the other nine?

TIDDLER

SHRIMP

CRAB

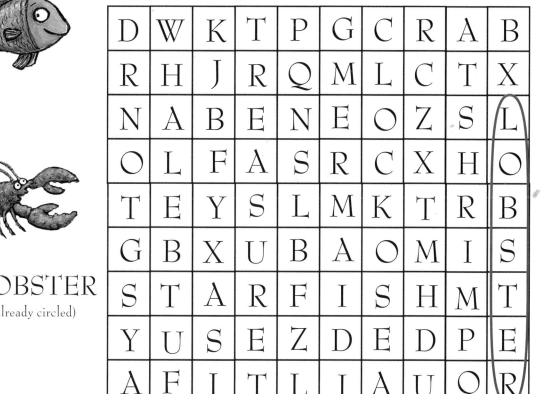

D	W	K	T	P	G	C	R	A	B
R	H	J	R	Q	M	L	C	T	X
N	A	B	E	N	E	O	Z	S	L
O	L	F	A	S	R	C	X	H	O
T	E	Y	S	L	M	K	T	R	B
G	B	X	U	B	A	O	M	I	S
S	T	A	R	F	I	S	H	M	T
Y	U	S	E	Z	D	E	D	P	E
A	F	I	T	L	I	A	U	Q	R
E	X	T	I	D	D	L	E	R	Z

LOBSTER
(already circled)

SEAL

STARFISH

MERMAID

WHALE

CLOCK

TREASURE

Jigsaws

There are two pieces missing from each jigsaw. They are in the sticker section. Can you find them and complete the scenes?

The Middle of the Ocean

Can you colour in this picture of the strange creatures Tiddler meets?

Spot the Difference

Can you spot ten differences between these two scenes?

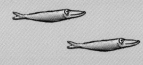

School Time

Can you help the fish with their lessons?

Can you count the starfish?

5

Can you spot the odd one out?

Can you do these sums?

2 + 2 = 4

4 - 1 = 3

2 + 3 = 5

Can you match the pairs?

Can you match the colours to the sea creatures?

Red   Pink   Yellow

Blue   Orange

Green

Can you trace Tiddler's name?

Tiddler

Can you write your own name?

Answers

Tiddler is Lost

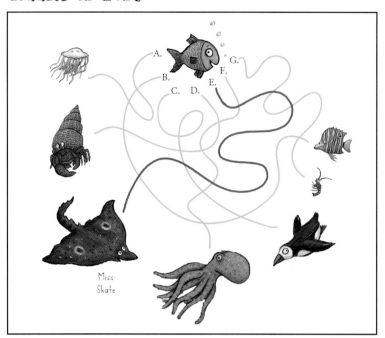

A.
B.
C. D. E.
F.
G.

Miss Skate

Tiddler's Wordsearch

D	W	K	T	P	G	C	R	A	B
R	H	J	R	Q	M	L	C	T	X
N	A	B	E	N	E	O	Z	S	L
O	L	F	A	S	R	C	X	H	O
T	E	Y	S	L	M	K	T	R	B
G	B	X	U	B	A	O	M	I	S
S	T	A	R	F	I	S	H	M	T
Y	U	S	E	Z	D	E	D	P	E
A	F	I	T	L	I	A	U	Q	R
E	X	T	I	D	D	L	E	R	Z

What's Next?

Spot the Difference

School Time

Odd One Out

Can you count the starfish?

5

Can you do these sums?

2 + 2 = 4

4 − 1 = 3

2 + 3 = 5